Loyola University Press
3441 North Ashland Avenue
Chicago, Illinois 60657

Translated from the Spanish by Roser Sala Claveras
and published in English with the permission of
Martín Casanovas Editor, Barcelona, Spain.

Library of Congress Cataloging-in-Publication Data
Puig, Enric.
Lord, I am one of your little ones.

Translation of: Señor, soy uno de tus pequeños
Summary: An illustrated collection of simple
prayers for a variety of situations. Includes
blank pages for the reader to write his/her own
prayers.
1. Children—Prayer-books and devotions—English.
[1. Prayer books and devotions] Bayés, Pilarín, ill.
II. Title.

BX2154.P8413 1987   242'.82   86-33810
ISBN 0-8294-0545-3

Lord, I am one of your little ones

Prayers for Children

by Enric Puig, S.J.
Illustrations by Pilarín Bayés

Loyola University Press
Chicago, Illinois

A Campion Book

6

Jesus said to them:

"Let the children come to me and do not hinder them. It is to just such as these that the kingdom of God belongs."

Mark 10:14

8

To all the children
who want to talk to Jesus
because He is their friend.

Do you know why we wrote this book?

We wrote this book to help you to pray, to talk to God, by yourself or with others: your dad, your mom, your brothers and sisters, your teachers, grandparents, priests, friends. When we pray with others we become a community. This book wants to help you to pray at any time and at any place you want to: at night, before going to bed; in the morning, before going to school; at Christmastime near the Baby Jesus; during your vacation . . .

The prayers we have chosen for this book are the spontaneous prayers of children eight to ten years old. This is how they have prayed. They want to share their prayers with you.

You'll find prayers to show that we are grateful to God for everything He does for us. Other prayers ask Him to help us to be better and to forgive us for whatever we haven't done well. There are also prayers about everyday events. At the end of the book you'll find some blank pages where you can add your own prayers to complete the book.

We would like all this to help you love God the Father, to follow the teachings of our Lord Jesus, and to let the Spirit lead you.

Let's start to pray . . .

14

We start with the Sign of the Cross.

In the name of the Father,
and of the Son,
and of the Holy Spirit.
Amen.

You can begin your prayers with these words. Ask someone to show you how to make the Sign of the Cross with your hand if you don't know how.

When the disciples asked Jesus to teach
them how to pray, He taught them this prayer:

Our Father, who art in heaven,
hallowed be thy name;
Thy kingdom come;
Thy will be done on earth as it is in heaven.

Give us this day our daily bread;
and forgive us our trespasses
as we forgive those
who trespass against us;

and lead us not into temptation,
but deliver us from evil.

It is good to follow Jesus' teachings and to
talk to the Father with this prayer every day.

You may also use it after saying one of the prayers in this book and then thinking for a while on its meaning.

If you want to pray to Mary, Jesus' mother
and our mother too, you may do it with this
prayer:

Hail Mary, full of grace,
the Lord is with you,
blessed are you among women
and blessed is the fruit
of your womb, Jesus.

Holy Mary, Mother of God,
pray for us, sinners, now
and at the hour of our death.
Amen.

And to praise God you may end your prayer
with this hymn:

Glory be to the Father
and to the Son and to the Holy Spirit;
As it was in the beginning,
is now, and ever shall be,
world without end.
Amen.

With thankfulness . . .

22

Thank you, Lord,

    for nature and the animals;
    for the beautiful rainbow after the rain;
    for the sun that gives us light and warmth
        and makes the plants grow;
    for the moon and the stars
        which shine at night;
    for the water that gives us life;
    for the fire that gives us heat;
    for the thoughts of men and women;
    and for all the friends who love us.

I thank you, Father,

    because I can see the beautiful things
      you have created.

I give you thanks, Lord,

    for the life and the love
    you have given to all people.

Thank you, Lord,

    for the love you give to us.
    Help us to share it with others.

Thank you, Lord,

    for today's outing.

Thank you, Lord,

    for all the living things around us.

Thank you, Lord,

> for the gift of imagination
> that you have given us;
> with it we can create many beautiful things.

Thank you, Lord,

> for everything you have graciously given to me,
> and to my friends,
> especially our happiness.

Thank you, Father,

> for giving us Jesus
> who taught us to tell the truth.

Thank you, Lord,

  for the beautiful day we had in our backyard.
    The tent made a very cozy home.

If we have failed in any way,
we ask you, Lord, to pardon us.

Father, you have given us the world
   and so many beautiful things!

Help us to thank you for it.
   We will work to keep it beautiful.

Thank you, Lord,

   for our parents, our teachers,
   and all the people who help us
   to live peacefully together.

Forgive us

   for the times
   we have not behaved towards them.

Help us

   to understand their work
   and love.

I give you thanks, Lord,

> because my mother is feeling better
> and because my father is now well.

I give you thanks also
> that we have fathers and brothers
> and because other children have them too.

Thank you, Lord,

> for my brothers and sisters;
> Thank you for my parents,
> and the love they have towards
> each other and towards me.

Help me to love them more.

Thank you, Lord,

    for the universe,
    for the earth and the sea,
    for the mountains, the valleys, and the
       rivers,
    for the farmers who plow the earth
       and harvest our food.

Thank you, Lord,

for the animals that keep us company,
   for the sun that gives us light,
   for the work that helps us live,
   for the trees that give us fruit,
     and the leaves that give us shade.

Lord,

   I thank you
      for all the children
      who help their parents.
   And I pray
      for all those who do not,
      so they may start helping.

Lord, I thank you

   for the strength you've given me
   to accept the classmates
      who get on my nerves.

I also thank you
   for giving us the Spirit of love
   to always wish for what is good.

We give you thanks, O Lord, our God,

for the trees on the land
and the fish in the sea,
for the sky, the water, and fire,
and for the gentle grass.

We give you thanks, O Lord, our God,

for the stars and the clouds,
for life and for death,
for the wind, the sun, and the moon.

We give thanks to the Lord, our God,
who has given us everything we have.

Thank you, Lord,

    for the chance to live
    and enjoy the things you give us.

I pray,

    that we may all learn to appreciate
    and to be thankful for all you give us.

Thank you, Lord,

    for the things you have given us,
        nature, the four seasons,
        the fruit of the trees,
        friendship among people,
        even among enemies.

I thank you, Lord,

    that when we have done something bad,
    we are able to be forgiven.

Lord,
   give us the strength to study
   and to pass our exams.

I thank you

   for nature,
      love,
      friendship,
      and peace.

I ♥ MEXICO

I want to pray

    for the gift of faith,
    so that I may thank God
    when my wishes are granted
    or when they are not.

Thank you, Lord,

    for the times I have asked forgiveness;

help me

    to play and to live
    without cheating
    and to always tell the truth.

Thank you, Lord,

for the food you have given us
and for the people who have prepared it.

Thank you, Father,

for the people who take pictures
of beautiful scenery.

I wish

that I could see those places
some day.

BRASIL

MATO-GROSSO

Thank you, Lord,

    for the beautiful day you have given me today,
and for letting me eat, play, and go to
    school.

38

We thank you, Father,

    that we can love the people around us,
    for all those who help us,
    for all the great and beautiful
    things you have given us.

Thank you, Lord,

    for my home, for my father's job,
    and for my family's health.

I would like to pray,

    for all those who don't have jobs,
    for all who are sick,
    and for those who don't have a home.

Thank you, Lord,

    for the mountains,
    for the trees and their fruit.

Thank you, Lord,

    for the sun that gives us light,
    and for the beautiful ocean
      where the light of the sun
      and the moon is reflected.

40

Thank you, Lord,

for the things we learn in school.
I've learned that I should not take money
from my father, my mother, or from anyone.
Help me to be strong when the temptation to steal
is almost too much to resist.

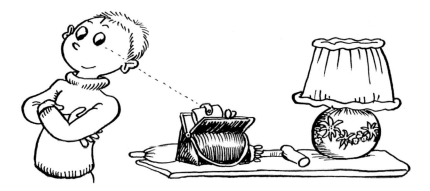

Thank you, Lord,

for the patience that the priests
and teachers have.

I pray

that others may follow their example.

Thank you, Lord,

for all the things you have given me,
especially my sight.

Please

help me to grow inside, to mature.

Help us to be better . . .

Lord,

help me to be aware of my mistakes
so I can ask for forgiveness.

Please, help me to do things better:
my school work,
my homework,
to make my bed every morning.

Father,

forgive me for being selfish.
   Sometimes I prefer what is easiest for me,
   instead of what is best for others.

When I ask for a favor,
   I always say that God wants us
   to love each other.

But when I am supposed to do a favor,
   I forget about love.

Teach me, when I'm asked for a favor,
to think as I do when I ask for one.

Teach me to share what I have,
even if it is not very much.

Jesus,

>   Forgive me
>   for the bad things I've done,
>   like when I told a lie,
>   or when I broke a plate
>   and blamed my sister for it.

Lord,

>   Forgive me
>   for the things I haven't done right:
>   for telling lies,
>   for thinking that I am always right
>   and my brothers are wrong,
>   for being lazy.

Please, help me to do better
and to say, "I'm sorry."

Lord,

forgive me for all the times
    I've left my work until the last minute,
    I haven't set the table;
Forgive me for losing my temper
    or hurting someone without meaning to.
Forgive me for the times I've been selfish
    with my friends or classmates.
Forgive me and teach me how to forgive,
    and help me to remember
      that when I forgive I act like Jesus.

Forgive me, Father,

    for all the bad things I've done:
        kicked a friend,
        made my mother angry, and my teacher,
        used foul language.

Thank you, Father,

        for all the good things I've done:
        helping a friend,
        letting someone use my pencil
        or play with my baseball.

Help me, Father,
to understand people,
and give me strength to love.

Help me to overcome my faults.

Forgive me, Lord,

> for having littered the street,
> and for spoiling some of the beautiful things
> that you have made.

Forgive me,

> for not being generous,
> for being a bother to others,
> for not always obeying my mother
> > when she asks me to do something.

Lord,

> I know I've been wrong
> when I hit my brother,
> when I got angry with my parents,
> and when I've told lies.

That's why I ask your forgiveness.
Thank you, Lord!

Jesus,

    I ask your pardon
        for all the times I've avoided responsibility
        and let my companions be blamed for things
        that I have done.

    And I thank you for all the times
        I had the courage to tell the truth.

Lord, forgive me

for all the times I got angry with my brother,
for the times I've cheated my friends,
and especially for the times I haven't done
    what I was asked to do.

Help me to overcome these faults of mine;
help me not to neglect my homework
by watching TV too much.

Everyday prayers . . .

Father,

I pray especially during the Christmas
   holidays,
when we celebrate the birth of Jesus,
that people may not suffer from hunger,
   cold, or sickness.

May there be happiness, peace, love,
hope, and joy in the whole world.

I ask you, Jesus,

>   to help us always think of you
>   when we are happy
>   or when we are sad.

I ask especially today when everyone at my house
is sad because grandpa died.

Lord,

>   help me to be aware of all the beautiful things
>   that come to me without cost:
>   joy, love, peace, friendship, and unity...

Lord,

>   give me the strength to study
>   and to do my work well,
>   not just quickly or carelessly.

Lord,

let there be love in my family,
especially today when my sister
is being christened.

Truth is beautiful,
and so is honesty.

It is far better to tell the truth
than to tell lies.

Lord,

help us to follow the right path,
the one that leads to you.

Lord,

I pray for everyone who is sick,
so they may get well.

I thank you, Lord,

for my parents,
and for the food you give us every day.

And I ask you, Lord,
to give me strength.

Lord, Jesus,

    I would like to pray
      for all the families
      who will not be able to celebrate
         Christmas
      because they have lost their jobs.

Lord,

    I pray that all the money spent on guns
    may be used to cure the sick
    and to help needy people.

My Father,
Father of all those who are living
and all who have died,
you watch us from heaven.

May your name be respected by everyone.

May we get to know your kingdom,
and everything good that you have created
in heaven and on earth.

Give us, Father, the best food,
the bread we have made with our own
efforts.

May everyone have something to eat,
and may we know how to ask you for it
every day.

Help us to be aware of our faults.

Forgive us the wrongs we have done,
as we forgive our friends.

Help us to avoid temptations
that would keep us from you.

Amen.

The disciples fell asleep three times
while Jesus was praying to the Father
to help him through the Passion.
They left him all alone.

I don't want to fall asleep.
I want to stay with Jesus.

Father, give me courage.

Lord,

 teach us to help one another,
 to be good to everyone,
 and to follow the way of the truth.

Lord,

 may the Holy Spirit always be with us,
 so that we may be like Jesus, our Savior.

Lord,

 whenever I feel lonely,
 may I think about you and feel close
 to you and to my friends.

Our Father,
and our friend!

Give us the strength
to help those who need us.

Help us to do good.

Don't leave us alone.

Help us to love everyone.

Give us work to do.

Teach us to share.

Forgive us our wrongs
as we forgive those
who have wronged us.

Teach us to follow Jesus' way,
    not to be selfish,
    not to quarrel with our friends.

Don't let us leave the right path.

Amen.

Father,

may everyone have food and shelter
this Christmas,
may we live in peace,
and may your love be always with us.

65

Lord, I ask you, please,

    may all men and women
      respect life and tell the truth,
    because it is your will.

Help me to be honest too.

Lord,
    help us to be strong
    so that as you died for us
    we may learn how to do things for others,
    and not to be selfish.

Lord,
    help me to do everything the best I can,
      to share my things,
      to treat them with care,
      and to respect other people.

Lord,

may this be a joyful Christmas,
with no sadness.

May there be peace in the world,
and may we share it with others.

May our faith in Jesus never weaken,
and may it extend through the whole world.

May we accept the difficulties in life.
Help us to overcome them.

May the needy people
be able to celebrate Christmas with
the same joy that we do.

Our Father,

I am your child,
and everyone is my brother and sister.

You are with all of us.

May your name be praised,
adored, and respected by everyone.

May your Spirit of love, goodness, and peace
be always with us.

Help us to do your will
always and everywhere.

Forgive the wrong we do
to our brothers and sisters.

Teach us to forgive as you do.

Help us to be good,
and help us to avoid evil, sickness,
hatred, and envy.

Amen.

Lord Jesus,

    may we always tell the truth
    so everyone may believe in you
    and trust may reign in the world.

Jesus,

    I would like to grow up
      in clean and unpolluted air.
    Teach grownups and children
    to keep nature beautiful.

Father, I pray,

   may we all have the spirit of love,
   kindness, humility, and sorrow for our sins.

We thank you for giving us your Spirit
   who makes us honest and loving.

Father,

   teach us to follow the example of Jesus.

   May we never look back on a life
   of selfishness and greed.

Lord,

   help me to feel the Spirit
   by being loving and friendly.

   When I do something wrong,
   may I always listen to the Spirit,
   who leads us to repentance.

Jesus,

> help me to be happy even when
> others receive more than I do,
> and help me to be humble and sharing.

Thank you,

> for all the times I didn't get upset
> when I was hurt by others.

Jesus,

Today I received my first communion
and I know that you are very close to me.
I want to ask you to help me.

Help me to love,
          to work,
          to study,
          to behave,
          to share,
          to have friends.

I do not know what prayer would be the best.
I almost don't know what to tell you, Lord Jesus.

I pray for love in life
and for peace in the world.

I pray that people may share with one another
and listen to one another,
and may not be selfish or dishonest.

I pray that everyone might know
the joy that you have given us!

Jesus,

   help us to work hard,
   to always tell the truth,
   even if we get scolded and into trouble.

To have the Spirit of love
is to love others.

Lord, I ask you,

   may the Spirit of love
   help us to be honest and trustful,
   and may it help all people
   as it helps us.

We feel the Spirit's strength
   when we behave,
   when we are not greedy but generous,
   and when we are happy with what we have.

That's why I ask you, Lord,
   to give me the strength of the Spirit.

My God,

   You are great and I am little,
   You move the sand in the desert,
   and I am just a grain of sand on the shore.

But I know that you love me
   and keep me close to you.

Remind me that you are always at my side,
even in difficult times.

Lord,

  help us not to interfere with
    Your Spirit's work in us,
  so we may love one another
    and always be happy in what we do.

Lord,

may wars stop.
They take people's lives,
lives that are so precious.

May we always live together in peace
and love one another.

Help us, Lord,

   to understand what our parents, our
      teachers,
   and our priests teach us.

Help us to practice those things too.

Thank you, Lord!

Lord,

   I ask You to help me overcome laziness
   when I do my homework and my chores.
   Help me to be kind to my brothers and sisters
   and not to talk back to my parents,
   or to anyone.

Help me, Jesus,

   to do things well,
   to be a good sport,
   to study,
   to behave better at home and in school.

Help me, Jesus,

    not to upset my mother,
    not to fight with my brother,
    not to do bad things,
    and not to quarrel with anyone.

I want to be happy
and to live in peace all my life.

Good our Father, I ask you

to give me the strength
to try to be like Jesus,
to know how to love Him.

Please help me to think of Jesus

this Holy Week and to remember
His death and resurrection.

83

I ask you, Father, if it may be,

that all people may be able to receive
the Bread of Life.
And may they offer themselves to you as
Jesus did.

And thank You for eternal life

which waits for us in heaven
if we offer ourselves to You
and to our brothers and sisters.

These are my own prayers . . .

The following blank pages are for you to write your own prayers, adding them to those written by the boys and girls who helped to write this book and who wanted to share their prayers with you.

You may also draw your own pictures, or you may color the ones that are already drawn in black and white. This way, the book will really be yours.

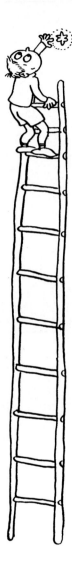

CONTENTS

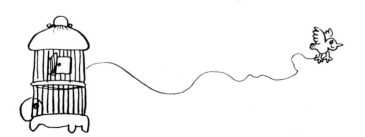